NOW YOU CAN PLAY

JAZZ

IMP

International MUSIC Publications

International Music Publications Limited
Griffin House 161 Hammersmith Road London W6 8BS England

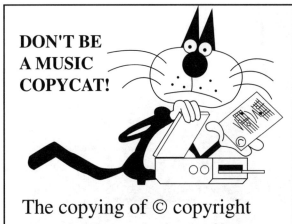

DON'T BE
A MUSIC
COPYCAT!

The copying of © copyright
material is a criminal offence
and may lead to prosecution.

Series Editor: Sadie Cook

Editorial & production: Artemis Music Limited
Design & production: Space DPS Limited

Published 1999

International
MUSIC
Publications

International Music Publications

England: Griffin House
               161 Hammersmith Road
               London W6 8BS

Germany: Marstallstr. 8
               D-80539 München

Denmark: Danmusik
               Vognmagergade 7
               DK1120 Copenhagen K

Carisch

Italy: Via Campania 12
               20098 San Giuliano Milanese
               Milano

Spain: Magallanes 25
               28015 Madrid

France: 20 Rue de la Ville-l'Eveque
               75008 Paris

NOW YOU CAN PLAY

JAZZ

Crazy Rhythm

Words by Irving Caesar
Music by Joseph Meyer and Roger Wolfe Kahn

Bright swing

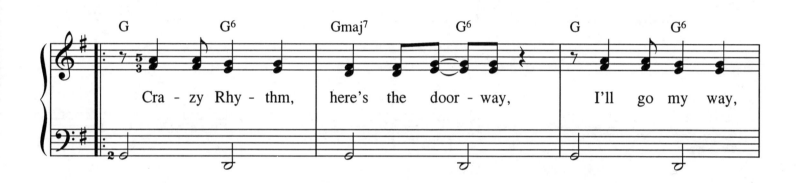

Cra - zy Rhy - thm, here's the door - way, I'll go my way,

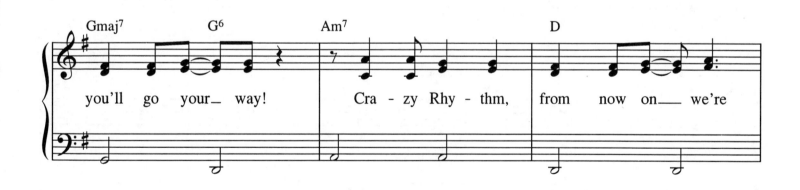

you'll go your_ way! Cra - zy Rhy - thm, from now on_ we're

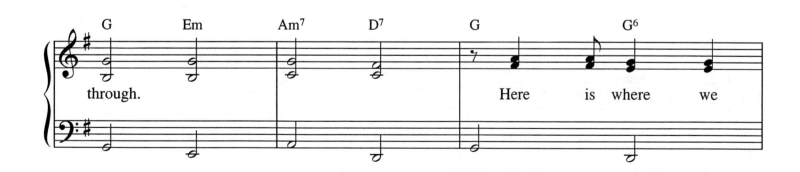

through. Here is where we

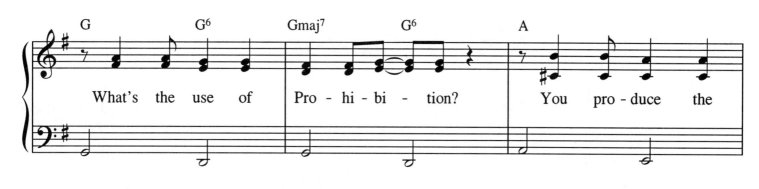

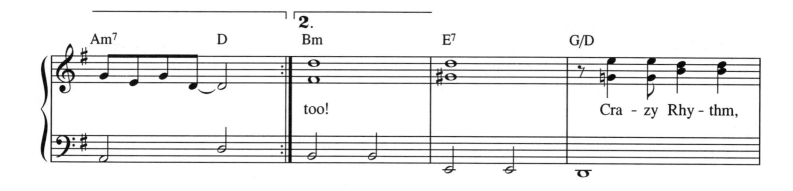

Ain't Misbehavin'

Words by Andy Razaf
Music by Thomas Waller and Harry Brooks

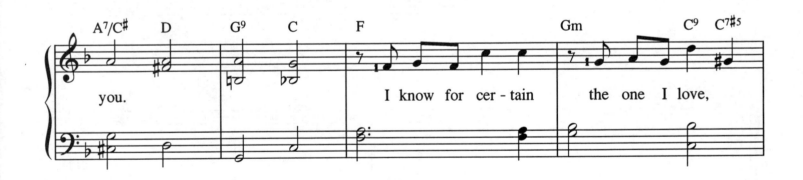

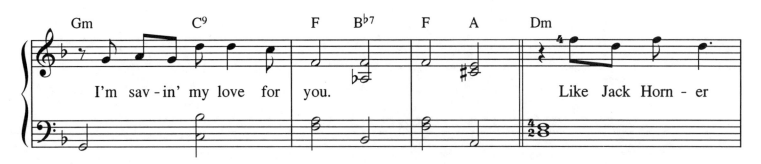

I'm sav-in' my love for you. Like Jack Horn-er

in the cor-ner don't go no-where what do I care, your kiss-es

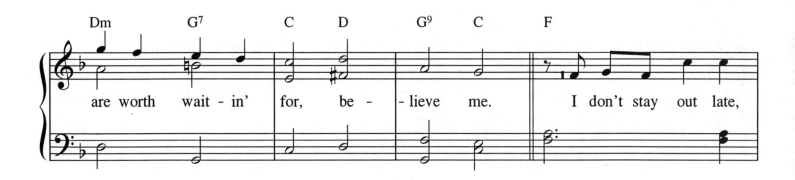

are worth wait-in' for, be - -lieve me. I don't stay out late,

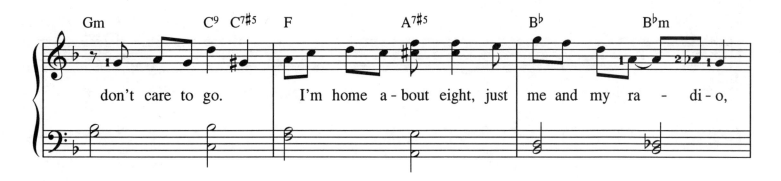

don't care to go. I'm home a-bout eight, just me and my ra - di-o,

ain't mis-be-hav-in' I'm sav-in' my love for you.

Don't Get Around Much Anymore

Words by Bob Russell
Music by Duke Ellington

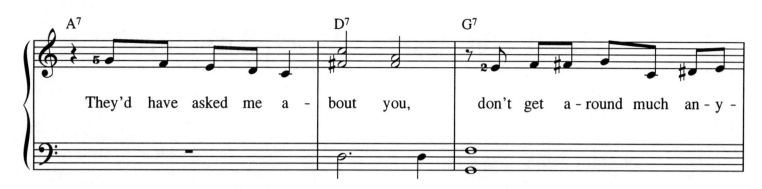

They'd have asked me a - bout you, don't get a - round much an - y -

more. Dar - - ling I

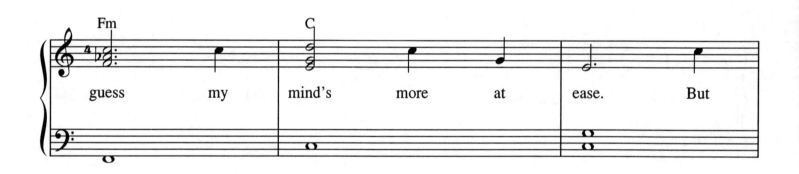

guess my mind's more at ease. But

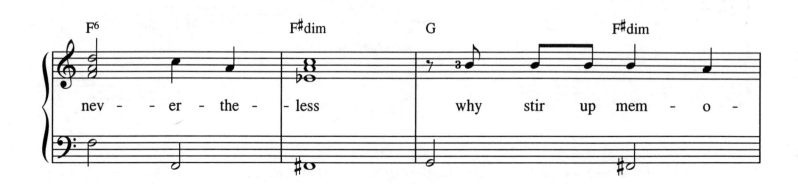

nev - - er - the - - less why stir up mem - o -

Dancing In The Dark

Words by Howard Dietz
Music by Arthur Schwartz

Rather slow (in 2)

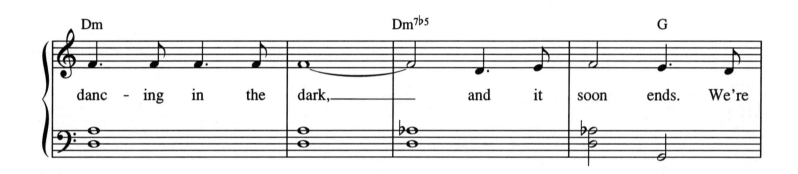

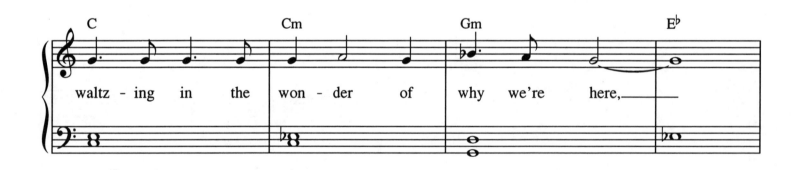

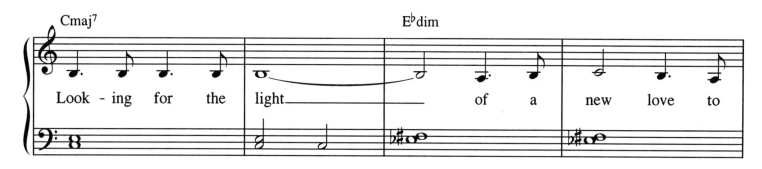

Look - ing for the light_____ of a new love to

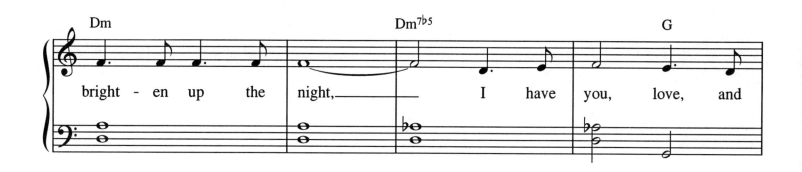

bright - en up the night,_____ I have you, love, and

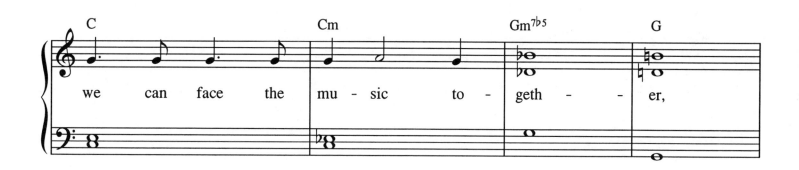

we can face the mu - sic to - geth - - er,

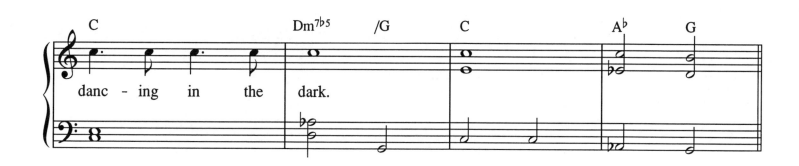

danc - ing in the dark.

What though love is old? What though song is old?

16

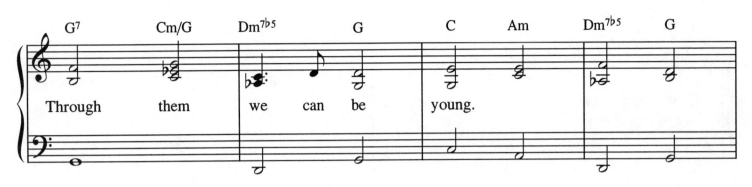

Through them we can be young.

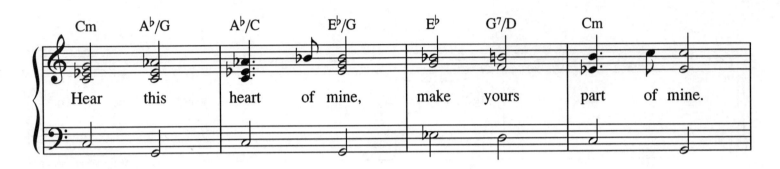

Hear this heart of mine, make yours part of mine.

Dear one tell me that we're one!

a tempo

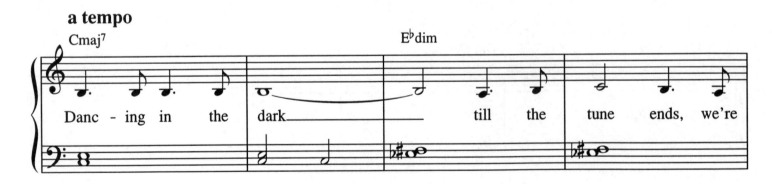

Danc - ing in the dark_____ till the tune ends, we're

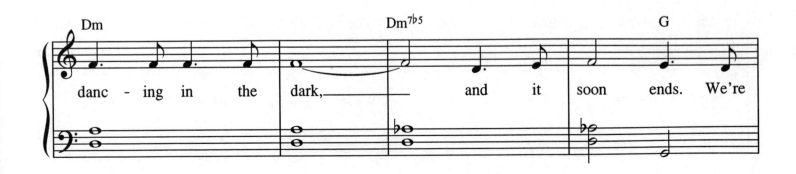

danc - ing in the dark,_____ and it soon ends. We're

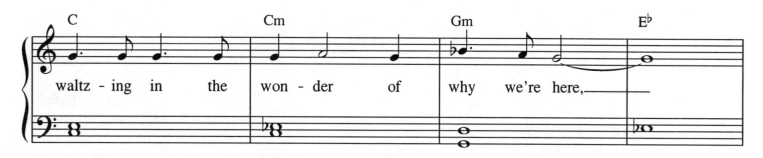

waltz - ing in the won - der of why we're here,____

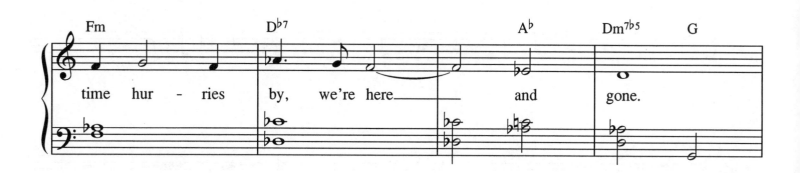

time hur - ries by, we're here____ and gone.

Look - ing for the light____ of a new love to bright - en up the

night,____ I have you, love, and we can face the mu - sic to -

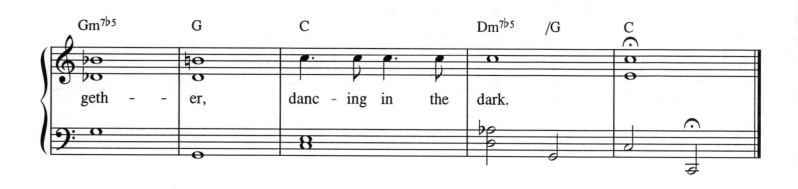

geth - - er, danc - ing in the dark.

Fever

Words and Music by
John Davenport and Eddie Cooley

Moderate swing (Swing ♪'s)

Nev - er know how much I love you, nev - er know how much I
Verse 2 see block lyric

care. When you put your arms a - round me, I get a

fe - ver that's so hard__ to bear. You give me fe - ver.

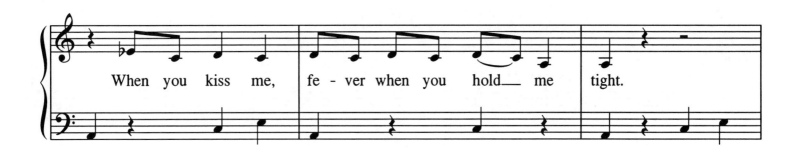

When you kiss me, fe - ver when you hold___ me tight.

E⁷

Fe - ver in the morn - ing, fe - ver all through the

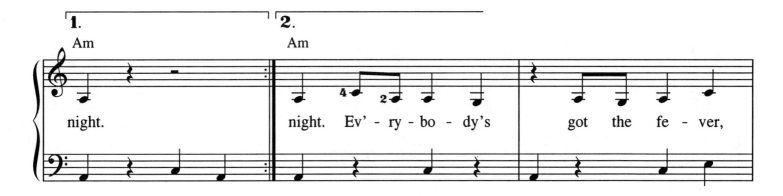

1. Am

night.

2. Am

night. Ev' - ry - bo - dy's got the fe - ver,

that is some - thing you all know. Fe - ver is - n't

E⁷

such a new thing, fe - ver start - ed long___ a - go.

Am

Now you've list-ened to my sto - ry, here's the point that I__ have

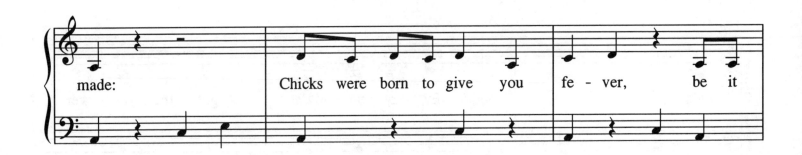

made: Chicks were born to give you fe - ver, be it

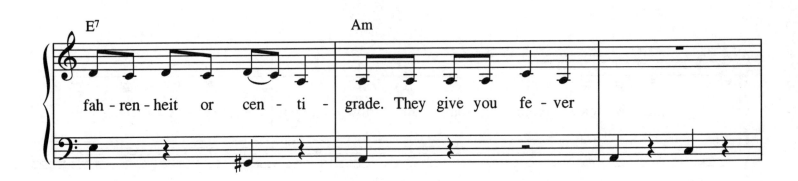

E⁷ Am

fah - ren - heit or cen - ti - grade. They give you fe - ver

when you kiss them, fe - ver if you live__ and learn.

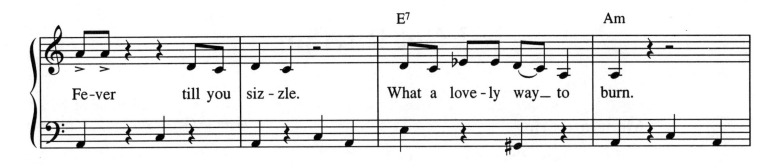

Slower

Verse 2
Sun lights up the daytime
Moon lights up the night
I light up when you call my name
And you know I'm gonna treat you right

You give me fever, etc

I Got Rhythm

Music and Lyrics by
George Gershwin and Ira Gershwin

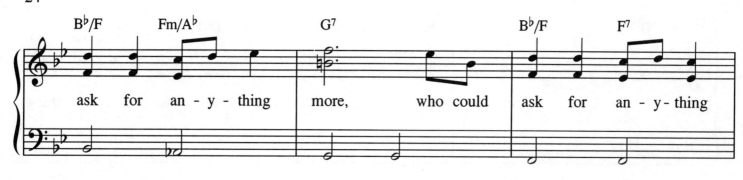

ask for an - y - thing more, who could ask for an - y - thing

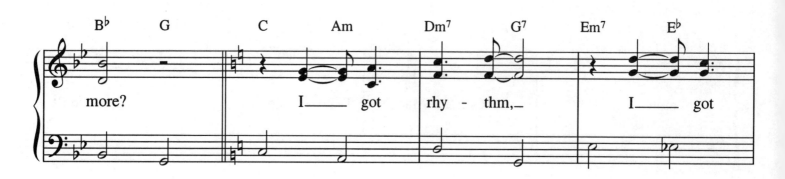

more? I___ got rhy - thm,___ I___ got

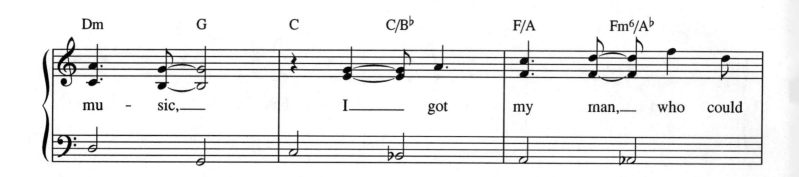

mu - sic,___ I___ got my man,___ who could

ask for an - y - thing more. I___ got dais - ies___

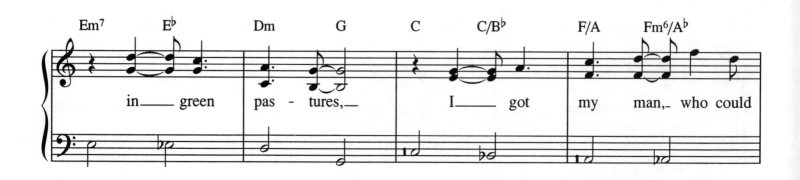

in___ green pas - tures,___ I___ got my man,___ who could

25

It's Only A Paper Moon

Words by Billy Rose and E Y Harburg
Music by Harold Arlen

love, it's a me - lo - dy played in a pen - ny ar - cade.

It's a Bar - num and Bai - ley world,— just as pho - ny as

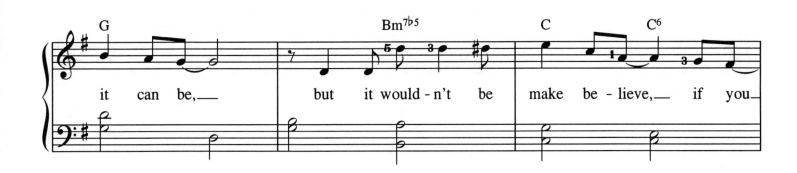

it can be,— but it would - n't be make be - lieve,— if you—

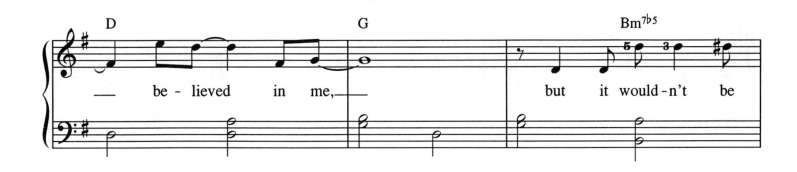

— be - lieved in me,— but it would - n't be

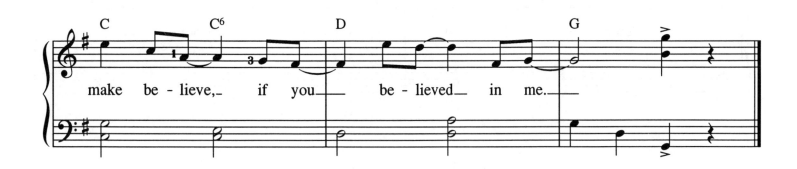

make be - lieve,— if you— be - lieved— in me.—

Jeepers Creepers

Words by Johnny Mercer
Music by Harry Warren

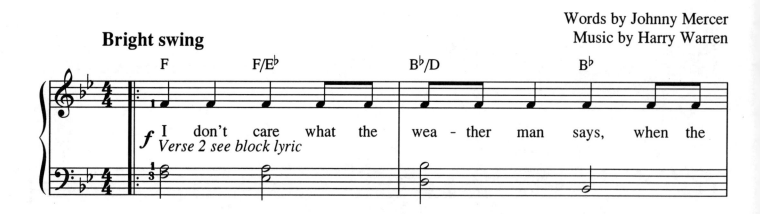

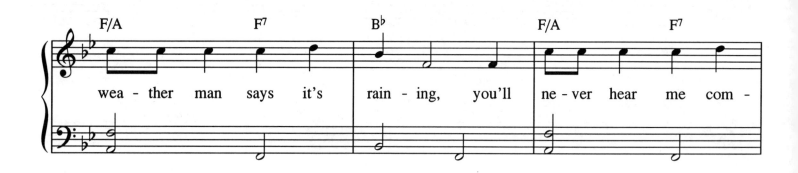

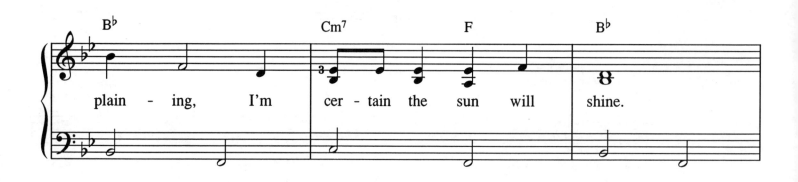

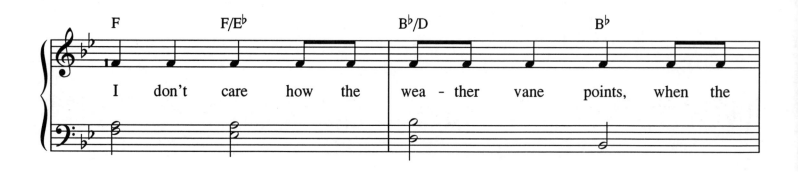

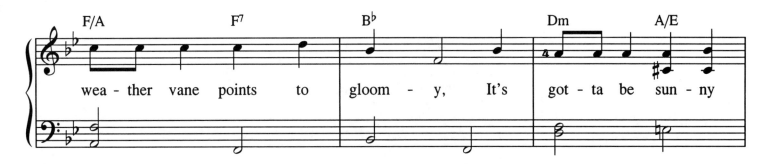

wea - ther vane points to gloom - y, It's got - ta be sun - ny

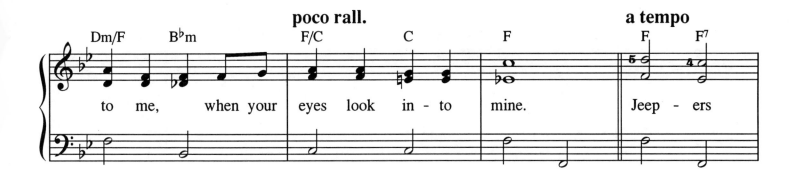

to me, when your eyes look in - to mine. Jeep - ers

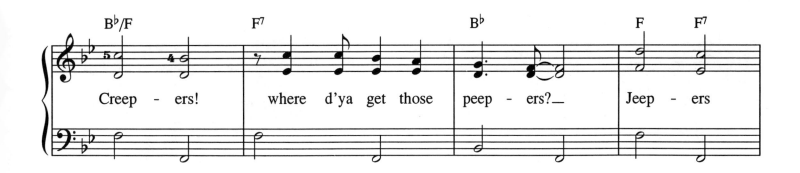

Creep - ers! where d'ya get those peep - ers?__ Jeep - ers

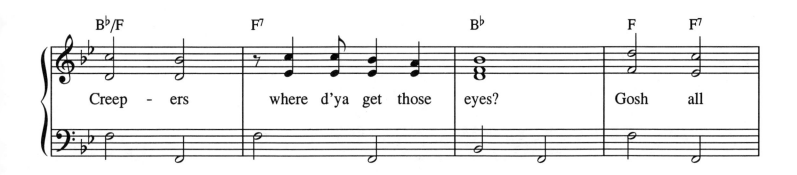

Creep - ers where d'ya get those eyes? Gosh all

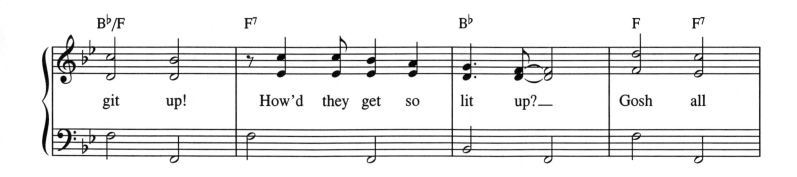

git up! How'd they get so lit up?__ Gosh all

eyes? eyes? Where d'ya get those eyes?

Verse 2
Sugar plum, I just haven't a chance
When you look round and show those eyes'es
You sure hand out great surprises
One melting look and I'm done
Somehow they lead me and do they lead
Down the road to complete disaster?
Each new day I'm fallin' faster
Your the rock I perish on

Jeepers Creepers, etc

34

Let There Be Love

Words by Ian Grant
Music by Lionel Rand

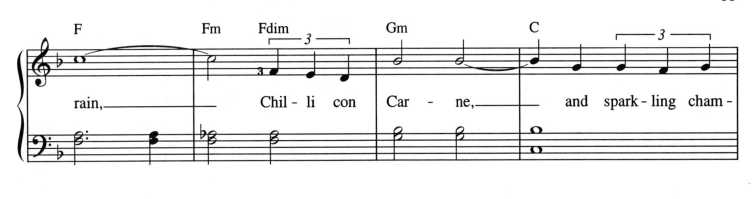

rain,_____ Chil - li con Car - ne,_____ and spark - ling cham -

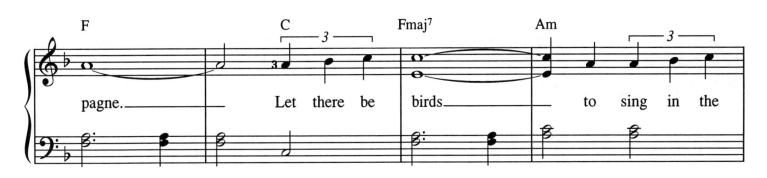

pagne._____ Let there be birds_____ to sing in the

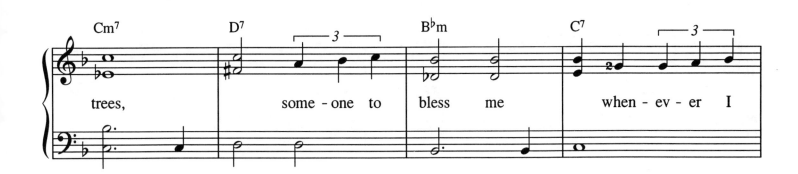

trees, some - one to bless me when - ev - er I

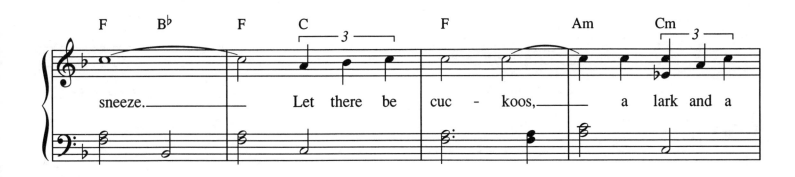

sneeze._____ Let there be cuc - koos,_____ a lark and a

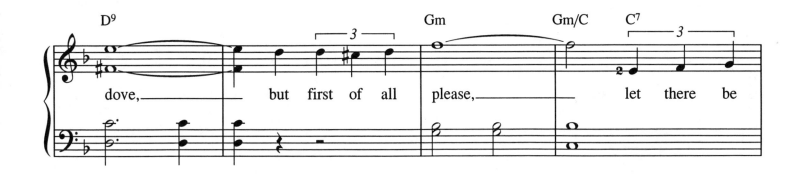

dove,_____ but first of all please,_____ let there be

36

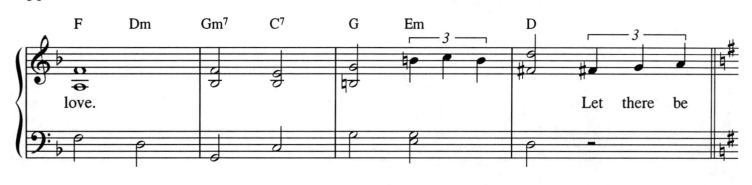

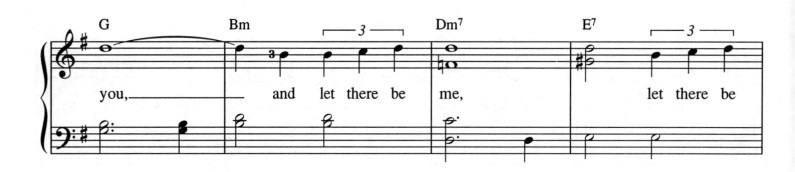

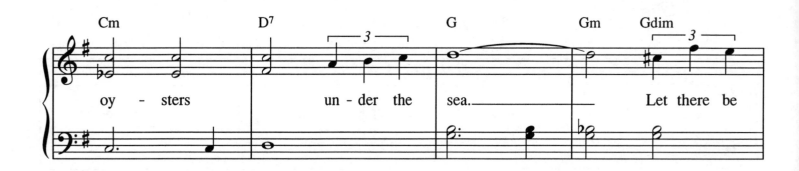

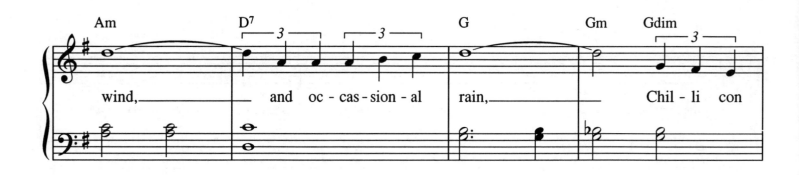

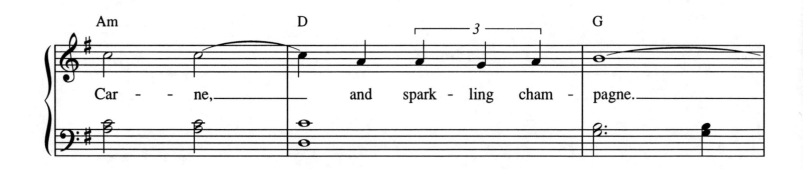

Summertime

Music and Lyrics by George Gershwin,
Du Bose and Dorothy Heyward and Ira Gershwin

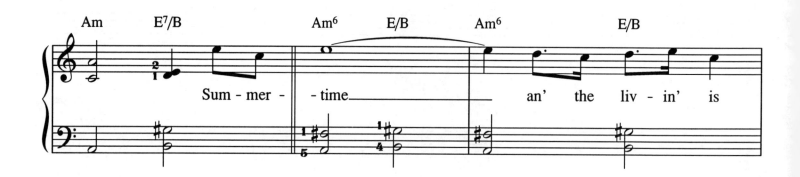

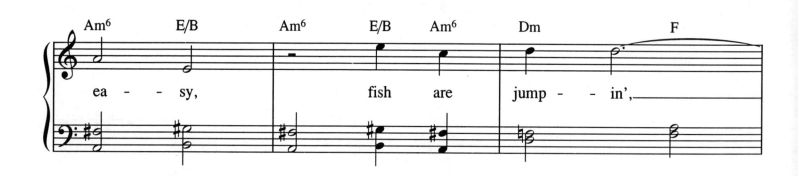

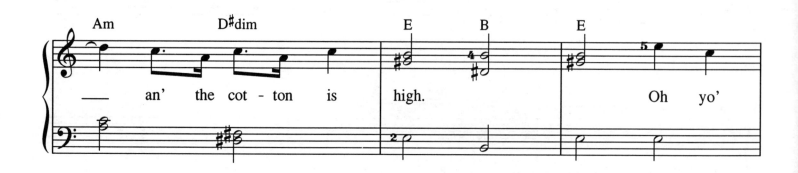

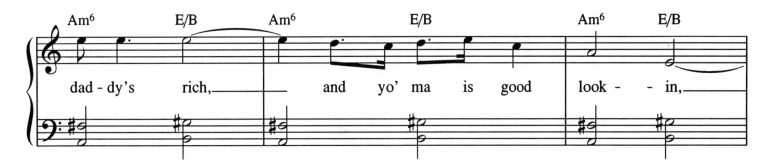

dad - dy's   rich,_____   and   yo' ma   is   good   look - - in,_____

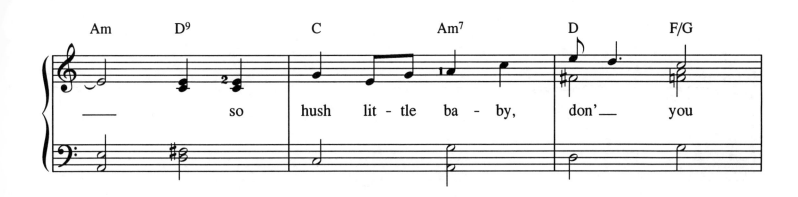

_____   so   hush   lit - tle   ba - by,   don'__   you

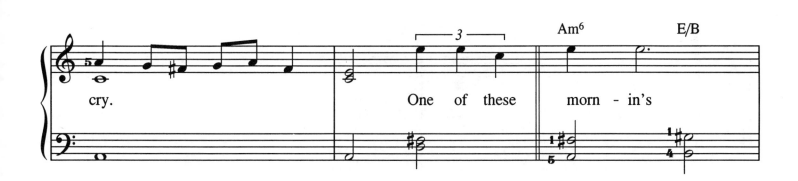

cry.   One   of   these   morn - in's

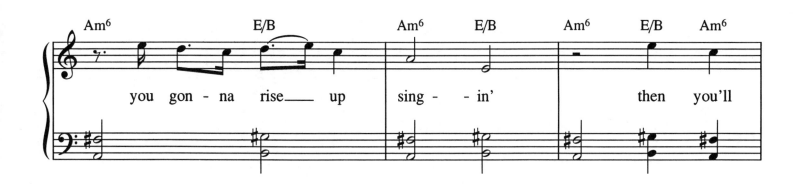

you   gon - na   rise____   up   sing - - in'   then   you'll

40

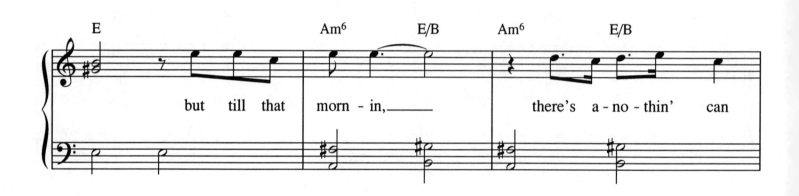

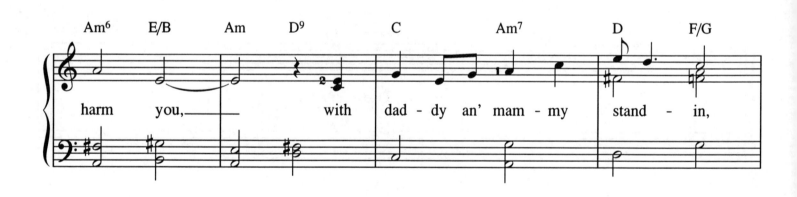

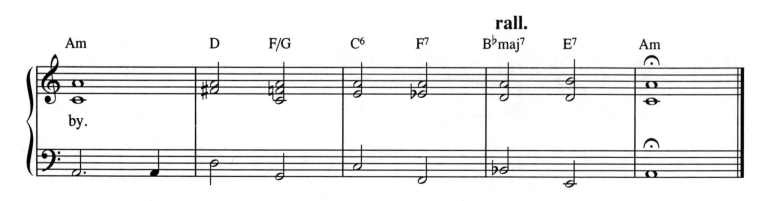